MAKE MONEY

FEW MINUTES A DAY TO BUILD A SIX-FIGURE BUSINESS WITH

K2 SYSTEM SPORTS BETTING

Very simple strategy for experts and beginners.

PAUL DENIS

TABLE OF CONTENTS

HOW TO EARN $20.000 IN 30 DAYS STARTING FROM $300

AND EARNING $20.000 A MONTH FOREVER

Yes, you read that right, how to earn $20,000 in 30 days starting from the initial sum of $300, well you'll win if you follow the simple instructions in this book and the videos I shot to explain better how to operate. Everyone can do it, even beginners, just be in legal age. So don't be discouraged if the topics covered don't seem to be within your reach, you'll be assisted by the site www.30days30.webnode.it which will give you the necessary support. It may happen that a small percentage of you'll lose the initial $300 due to a negative series that, in very rare cases, could occur. But it's possible to start again from the beginning so it is only a matter of anticipating a few dollars more and that's it. Someone instead could get a sum of less than $20,000 but still have the necessary instructions to earn a good monthly salary for the following years. In any case, the majority of you will succeed in the enterprise, and if all goes well, you'll earn even more, all this must give you the right charge to start and not give up.

A key piece of advice I give you is not to share with anyone what learn from this book because, if many other people win, bookmakers, in the long run, could switch to countermeasures and you could lose out too by not being able to play these systems anymore.

Before going into the real earning method, remember that at the end of the path, there are the $20,000 you'll get, probably in 30 days, maybe more or maybe less! And that you'll continue to increase monthly for life, so don't give up at first hitch or topic you don't understand, at least let yourself be helped by someone more familiar with the subject, but don't give up!

I state, however, that I'm not a professor, and I'm not native English, so I apologize if I made some mistakes in the multiple exposures. All I know I owe to the experience and the various self-taught studies I have done over the years.

LET'S GET TO THE POINT

The types of investment that I'll talk about in this book have profitability expressed with a multiplier coefficient "odd" or "coeff," always greater than 1.

Practically, investing, for example, $100 on an odd 1.8 in the positive case, we'll have obtained $100 x1.8 = $180 with a net profit of $80. These investments will take place at very short intervals, for example, one per minute, as happens in the double chance game of roulette, or medium close, one or two per day, as in the case of a sequence of sports bets.

When the odd is approximately 2.00, we'll call the play "double." Initially, we'll increase the capital by using a simple roulette system. Then when it comes to having substantial capital, we'll focus more on betting.

After 30 days, instead, we'll orientate ourselves towards mixed strategies, gains at the roulette, bets at low coeff, or doubling which every month get more victories than defeats always to obtain a monthly profit. Depending on the amount of the daily stake, you'll decide how much to earn monthly.

THE ECONOMIC PROGRESSIONS

Now let's look at the various economic progressions that exist that allow us to manage the capital and then the ones we'll use to make the most of the indications of the various systems illustrated in this book. The best-known ones can be summarized in these five:

1) Masaniello Table

2) Doubling

3) Fibonacci sequence

4) D'Alembert progression

5) Fixed stake

And finally our custom upright:

- 6) 30days progression

Now examine the progressions mentioned above in detail.

1) The first economic progression, called Masaniello (from the name of its developer), used above for coefficients higher than 2.5/3.0. It consists in always having under control what has been spent and what is expected from the next possible gain by updating everything in case of loss. After a series of negative and positive events, we look at the budget and decide how much to invest in the next operation based on what is expected to be achieved to reach the goal we have set ourselves. To facilitate the

practical implementation of this strategy, it is advisable to prepare an excel file with the programming of the cells to calculate the progression automatic. On the internet, you can find excel sheets to download for free. Then we'll find in a box the budget of what we played, in another, we'll put the amount we are going to play with relative coeff and then the new budget in case of a positive outcome. You'll understand better if and when you'll use it.

2) The second progression is called the Doubling and is used exclusively with coeff = 2. A basic capital to be invested must be fixed, which will double in the event of a loss, while in the event of a win, the base capital will be returned. For example, you set a base of $5, if you lose you invest $10, if you lose you invest $20, if you lose you invest $40, if you earn you go back to the base $5. This progression should be used when losses are rare, and above all, they are not close to each other because a series of prolonged losses would lead to the failure of the operation as the amount to invest would be too high.

3) The third progression is that of the Fibonacci series, which is starting from 1 sum the last number with the second to last to get the new sequence number: 1,1,2,3,5,8,13,21,34,55,89 etc. To the original Fibonacci sequence, however, we'll remove the first 1, and therefore ultimately, we'll have: 1, 2, 3, 5, 8, 13, 21, 34, 55, 89 and so on. This progression is ideal for investments that are close to 2. You'll need to invest in an increase in case of loss of capital and a decrease in case of a positive outcome. I will make a practical example to understand better how to apply it.

We invest 1 on a coeff 2, which means that it will give us an active of 1 in case of a positive outcome, but we lose. In the next session, we invest 2. If we lose, we invest 3, and if we win, we invest 2 or go ahead in progression if we lose and back if we win. In every section of the progression in which we find ourselves. This allows us always to have active.

You can also double up to the second or third shot lost to return to 1 in case of winning if we find in the doubling and so continue to add the last two numbers. In this way we'll have 1,2,4 - 6,10,16,26,42 etc. in this case it returns to 1 if it wins while we are betting 2 or 4, or 1,2,4,8 - 12,20,32,52 etc. it returns to 1 if it wins while we are betting 2, 4 or 8. But for this progression, there is a need to have a big starting capital. Finally, we can modify the starting unit based on the capital we put into play and then change the progression based on this unit. If we have a capital of $500 we could decide to start from 5 and not from 1, in this case, we have to multiply the numbers of the progression by 5, for the basic Fibonacci we get 5,10,15,25,40,65,105, etc. if we then have a capital of $750. We decide to set the base stake at 7. We multiply by 7 and so on.

4) Then we have the D'Alembert progression that is applied when, in the statistics of the investment with events having coeff 2, positive events occur in a number greater or equal than the negative events and consists in increasing one unit in the event of loss and is decreasing by one unit in case of gain. Example. An initial investment of $1, if you lose, you invest $2, if you lose you invest $3, if you win you invest $2, if you lose you invest $3, if you win you invest $2, if you win you invest $1. At the end of this progression, we'll probably have multiplied our initial capital by 1.5. Give excellent results in betting with coeff 2 (so-called

doubling) because, by experience, the winnings are always higher than the losses.

5) Then we find the Fixed stake that expects to always use the same sum for all the events. And without increasing, which is used when in the statistics of the investment, we have positive events in a greater number than the negative ones and certainly with a coeff of 2 or higher. For example, if we have 30 events with an average coefficient of 2.5 with an investment of $500 for each event and 20 earnings and 10 losses occur on average, we'll have spent $15,000 (500 x 30) and will have received $25,000 (500x2.5 = 1,250x20) with a profit of $10,000, and we'll never need to increase the bet. The pessimist on duty will immediately have thought: "but who has $15,000 to risk?" This pessimist, however, overwhelmed by his negativity, didn't think that the winnings could come already from the first event for which he will have spent only $500. Or at the limit, if the winnings arrive after the second or the third blow, risks a maximum of $1500. But no more. So if you're one of those pessimists, I suggest you start thinking differently because we don't risk more than the initial $300 here. If you think that $300 is too much, look for a better investment of 100,000% per year. In any case, we could adopt the Fixed capital when we have increased the capital a lot, and we'll make daily sports bets.

6) In the end, we have the 30days progression is an upright created by me, which we'll use in the game of double chance at the roulette and which is a mixture of Fibonacci, doubling and D'Alembert. This riser allows you not to burn the whole case in case of negative series that are not too long, to those no riser can resist. In practice the doubling is done up to the tird error that is 1,2,4,8 then in loss, it increases of +5, of +7, of +10, of +15, of

+22, of +33, and so on (with some rounding) while in winning it goes back of two positions and not of one like in D'Alembert or Fibonacci. So at a loss we'll have this sequence: 1,2,4,8 - 13,20,30,45,67,100. When you win, you go back 2 from 9 upwards, so for example, if we win when we bet 44, we'll play 20 in the next round. We'll decide to return to play 1 when at the end of the negative series, we'll be back to the starting capital +1. We must never forget to play even on zero in the event of a prolonged loss and, therefore, a high bet to recover in the event of a sortie of zero.

In this book, I'll explain when using the various types of progressions depending on the investment we are making in order always to obtain the maximum profit.

THE CASINOS

Now I talk about casinos. All online casinos are fine. In my opinion, however, the best casinos are those that have the Evolution Gaming platform as it allows you to instantly view up to 500 previous numbers and then immediately make the necessary statistics based on the numbers released to make the decision on the game sequence to be adopted so you should look for the casinos in your country that have such a platform. You can also play on the other casinos you find on the net, but in this case, you'll have to mark the last 30/40 releases by hand to see the double chance statistic. Some casinos have no zero roulette that are very positive when playing on double chances.

Said that we must take into account the fact that up to a certain sum won that could be $10,000/15,000 the casino does not notice you, but if you win systematically it could block you and cancel the account, so the advice is to open different accounts on the various casinos in to play on so many and not always on the usual which could, therefore, block you. You can also open accounts in the name of your close relatives, but in this case, you must have more than one computer so that the IP address is not the same since the casino software sees it and understands that you are the same person with two different identities. It is not a crime, but the casino will block one of the two accounts. Furthermore, when you win, it is advisable to withdraw as much as possible, leaving only the amount you need to play next time. If you lose, you'll go to recharge.

Real casinos are also good; just write the last ones released before starting the sequence.

About real casinos and live roulette, in general, I want to debunk the various myths and legends circulating about them. It is said that roulette is made up, that the croupiers succeed in throwing the ball where they want them, that when the table is all pointed the ball deliberately falls on the number where there are no bets. Well, none of this is true for the simple fact that the ball spins freely before the eyes of dozens of people if it had any strange or magnetized behavior, do you think we wouldn't all notice it? And then with all the rounds do you think that a croupier can predict and direct the area where to drop it? It is pure madness. I have several croupier friends, and when I told him this thing, they started laughing. By definition, the roulette is made up in itself because there are always different and strange sequences of numbers that don't follow any statistics, chaos reigns, so the dealer always wins.....or almost, ;)))).

Having said this it is important to add that we must not play to the infinite because the negative series of prolonged errors that make you lose everything is lurking and therefore once the objective is realized you must close and resume at the next established session, there is no winning system to the roulette, this must be clear.

SPORTSBOOK

What no one says but must be very clear is that it's impossible to lose at sports betting. You'll say that I'm crazy, but it is not so, in fact, who bets knows that sooner or later he will win, but be careful, only who have accurately scored all the sum played up to that moment and in the last bet will have staked such an amount to recover the losses and going into profit will win, all the others will not be able to cover the expenses and will continue to replenish the funds of the bookmakers.

Sport Bets are three types:

singles, when we bet on only one event of a match;

multiple, when we bet on more than one event of several games;

systems, when we bet on several games with some conditions, for example, 5 points on 6 events so that if we fail 1 game, we win the same or with fixed games and others to run with various possibilities of error.

The various types of bets that are used in the majority are 1, X or 2 which means respectively the home team wins, draws or wins the visiting team; then there are the double chances, that is two combined results 1x, x2 and 12. So 1X means the home team win or draw. Or the over that can be 0,5 1,5 2,5 3,5 etc. and that gives a positive result in the case in which in the match more of the goals on which we have bet is scored. Over1.5 means that at the end of the match, 2 or more goals will have been scored regardless of which team scores. In the same way, there are the under or less goals scored compared to the prediction. Then there are the multigols1-3, 1-4, 2-4, etc. also half match 1ST or 2nd. Then there are so many of them combined that it is impossible to treat all so those who are not experts must get help, at least initially from some friend who understands us or copies the play and takes her to the agency to make her play. However, I enclose a small handbook of predictions at the end of the book.

Every available event to bet on has a coeff multiplier of the amount bet. In the case of a multiple, the coeff multiply among themselves so if we have a multiple of two games, one of which with odd 1.45 and one with odd 1.55 we'll have a final odd for the multiple one equals to 2.25 (1.45 x 1.55) to which is added a bonus when generally more than 3 games are played.

You can find dozens of "Tipster" groups or singles on Facebook, Telegram or Instagram that give predictions, even for free, which you can use for bets useful for achieving our goal. Generally, however, they give doublings, that is, at odd 2 or lower, but you can also find who goes beyond doubling. If they have a cost, you have to pay it because they will still make you a profit. The problem with these Tipsters is that they give the bet a few hours before the start of the matches, so you have little time to do it, organize yourself. I will publish daily some multiple 2.00 and 3.00 average odd, from 7 to 9 combination that you can also join together on my free website www.30days30.webnode.it about European and Asian championship. It at least 24 hours before the start of the games so you'll have plenty of time to play them. In any case, reliability is the same, I'm not better than other Tipsters, so you are free to use the ones you consider most appropriate based on the statistics.

To know the results of the matches, you can go to www.scoreboard.com   www.futbol24.com   or www.sofascore.com. Then www.diretta.it especially for European, Asian and South American results.

Anyway, I wanted to let you know others way to get doublings that are not singles or multiples of two or three matches with simple predictions that generally give the Tipster because in my opinion sooner or later the bookmakers will set a minimum odd higher than 2.00 for the sport bets seen that many people are earning too much with bets. With other game modes that I'll illustrate, you can also take multiple winnings so that they don't only double, but they multiply by 4 or by 8, and this can be advantageous in the bets that aim at the high average of the winnings possibly at fixed capital.

The first method to have a doubling in a different way from what the Tipsters usually do is to play two multiples at odd 4. This is obtained with two groups of 2/3 or more matches together or by combining 4 doublings in 2 couples. To double, just win one, but sometimes you can win both and become a quadruple. So staking $50 on 2 multiple with odd 4, for a cost of $100, we'll win $200 if we get one and $400 if we get both, with a profit of +$100 in the first case and +$300 in the second one. This method allows us to mistake one or two matches and win the same. If the two multiples have slightly different odd between them, the amount of wagered must be adjusted so that they give the same profitability/gain.

Then you can play by error correction. This method is also good for those players who play a lot of matches and generally make only a mistake and then swear. Once the base column has been made, which for doubling should have a minimum odds of 7/8, all the predictions are corrected one by one by putting the error in place of the base one. To correct a combined result such as 1x+over1.5, for example, we have put first the 2 and then the under1, 5, and so we'll correct it with two bet columns and not with one. The basic multiple and the various multiple corrections that we'll make must be of an amount, such as to have a yield that is twice the total amount staked.

To explain better, I give a practical example:

Base		1st Error		2nd Error		3rd Error		4th Error		5th Error	
1	1.50	X2	2.50	1	1.50	1	1.50	1	1.50	1	1.50
1	1.50	1	1.50	X2	2.50	1	1.50	1	1.50	1	1.50
1	1.50	1	1.50	1	1.50	X2	2.50	1	1.50	1	1.50
1	1.50	1	1.50	1	1.50	1	1.50	X2	2.50	1	1.50
1	1.50	1	1.50	1	1.50	1	1.50	1	1.50	X2	2.50
	7.59		12.66		12.66		12.66		12.66		12.66
Stake $10		Stake $6		Stake $6		Stake $6		Stake $6		Stake $6	
Win $76		Win $76		Win $76		Win $76		Win $76		Win $76	

Another way that I use very frequently is to play the surprises, that is predictions in countertrend that have high odd on average close to 8.00, and play the bets in number the half of the odd that is 4, or play in number 6 if we want to get 50% instead of the doubling. Many surprises occur every day and they are, for example, the victory of visitors team "2" with odd on average 8.00 (7.00/9.00). We can also get this odd with combo or multiple predictions, and then if we play odd close to 12 we can play 6 of them, the important thing is that we play predictions at very similar odd and that we play bet tickets in the number equal to half the average odd. So if the average odd is 16, we'll play 8 bet tickets. You can find some surprises on my free website.

So if we play $10 on 4 bet tickets with odd 8.00 each, we'll spend $40, and we'll win $80 if we catch one, thus obtaining a doubling, and $160 if we take 2 getting a quadruple. If we are content to multiply by 1.5 instead of doubling, we can play 5 or 6 surprise bets with at odd 8.00 to have more chances of winning in the expectation of taking 2 and making a bang. If we want to exaggerate, we can make a system to do 2 points on 9 or more surprises match that wins if we get 2 of these, but that wins a lot if we win more than two. In fact, with 9 matches, there will have 8+7+6+5+4+3+2+1 = 36 combinations of couples at average odd 64 (8.00*8.00), but still be assured because this system will do it automatically, so if we play the $3 bet by combination we'll have spent $108. We'll win $192 if we make 2 points that will become $576 if we make 3 points and even $1152 if we take 4 of them. Example for 7 matches combined in 21 couples:

1.Match 1 - Match 2;	2.Match 1 - Match 3;	3. Match 1 - Match 4;	4. Match 1 - Match 5;
5.Match 1 - Match 6;	6. Match 1 - Match 7;		
7.Match 2 - Match 3;	8.Match 2 - Match 4;	9. Match 2 - Match 5;	10. Match 2 - Match 6;
11.Match 2 - Match 7;			
12.Match 3 - Match 4;	13.Match 3 - Match 5;	14. Match 3 - Match 6;	15. Match 3 - Match 7;
16. Match 4 - Match 5;	17. Match 4 - Match 6;	18. Match 4 - Match 7;	
19. Match 5 - Match 6;	20. Match 5 - Match 7;		
21. Match 6 - Match 7;			

There are days when lots of surprises occur; then, in the long run, this play can be very profitable. Finally, the first-half/second-half results of match that have the home team odd 1.30/1.50, which we can play 2 in the first halftimes and 1 or X second half (2/X or 2/1), are very profitable. In the first case, the odd are about 23/24.00 and in the second about 15/16.00. We could play for example a system of 8 games with both possibilities for each game, 2/1 or 2/X, and set 2 points, which are 28 combinations, but playing an amount per column that isn't too high. When we win 3 of these, the profit will be very high.

Another method is to opt for an odd close to 12/13.00 and obtain it by joining two groups of matches with a total odd of 3/4.00. So prepare 6 groups with matches all different from each other whose total odd of the single group is close to 3/4.00 and combine them with two by two to have 6 multiples of 6 matches each that also get the bookmaker's bonus, that generally on 6 games is 1.10. In this way, you'll win if you settle two or more groups. I make an abstract example with 4 groups of 3 matches each to make you understand better.

Group A: match 1 odd 1.50, match 2 odd 1.50, match 3 odd 1.50. total odd 3.38 (1,50x1,50x1,50=3.38).

Group B: match 4 odd 1.50, match 5 odd 1.50, match 6 odd 1.50. total odd 3.38.

Group C: match 7 odd 1.50, match 8 odd 1.50, match 9 odd 1.50. total odd 3.38.

Group D: match 10 odd 1.50, match 11 odd 1.50, match 12 odd 1.50. total odd 3.38.

Now we combine various groups 2 per 2 to get 6 multiples:

1)A-B; 2)A-C; 3)A-D; 4)B-C; 5)B-D; 6)C-D.

Multiple 1) match 1, match 2, match 3, match 4, match 5, match 6. Total odd 12.57 (within bonus of1.10).

Multiple 2) match 1, match 2, match 3, match 7, match 8, match 9. Total odd 12.57.

Multiple 3) match 1, match 2, match 3, match 10, match 11, match 12. Total odd 12.57.

Multiple 4) match 4, match 5, match 6, match 7, match 8, match 9. Total odd 12.57.

Multiple 5) match 4, match 5, match 6, match 10, match 11, match 12. Total odd 12.57.

Multiple 6) match 7, match 8, match 9, match 10, match 11, match 12. Total odd 12.57.

If we stake $10 on each multiple, we'll spend $60, and we'll win $126 for each one we settle. One in the case we settle 2 groups, and then we'll have doubled, and 3 in the case we settle 3 groups then a +$318, which is not bad. Think about getting the 4 groups. The delirium.

In practice, however, we don't have odd so similar so we could make multiples of 5 or 7 matches with different odd but will be sufficient to adjust the amount staked on each multiple so that they have the same profitability.

However, I must point out that the fact of making 4 groups with odd 3/4.00 not be binding, so who wants can make more or less groups and combine them two by two, the important thing is that winning one single or multiple gives more or less the double of total amount spent.

Indeed, it is a bit difficult, but once you become familiar, it can be a good way to win big sums.

I conclude the topic with the game that I think is more convenient, and that are two bets at odd 3.00 of the same amount that allows us to multiply the capital by 1.5 if we win one and multiply by 3 if we win both. The two predictions with odd 3.00 you can be found on my free site.

For betting, it's also convenient to have more accounts on various authorized online bookmakers so that if you have to play, for example, $5000, you can split the bet into 5 and make it on 5 different sites. The best bookmakers in U.S. are Bovada, 5Dimes, Intertops and many others. Or you can play in the authorized physical betting agencies that you find in the area. Also, in this case, if you have to stake a lot of money, you'll bet in more than one agency, so you don't stake too much in the same agency. Who has less experienced can copy the predictions given by the Tipsters or which find on my website and show it to the employee of the Sports betting agency to play.

Regarding both online casinos and sports bet, I advise you don't have to take the welcome bonuses of the various websites because you have to be play that in various ways to be consolidated that could condition you in your games. If you aren't an expert, you'll be without a bonus anyway.

STARTING PLAY MODE

The economic scheme that we'll apply initially is that of increasing all the possessed capital of a fixed daily percentage, always putting in stake all the same capital. We'll, therefore, try to increase the capital by a minimum of 30% every day. Starting from $300, in 5 days, we'll reach about $1100 ($300 x1.3 x1.3x1.3x1.3 x1.3 = $1100). This first step will be achieved with the roulette. In the following 10 days, we'll try to earn $500 for day, and this will be done with sports betting and the roulette, so we'll increase the capital by +$5000 for a total of $6100. At this point, we can withdraw $1,100 to savor the first taste of victory. Done, this will remain 15 days to produce the $15,000 missing with a strategy that will surprise you. Since generally, you can enter in the roulette table with a maximum of $1000, it would be risky and annoying to stay there for hours trying to win $1600 a day. So we'll use the roulette to make only small gains, which will still be useful, but most of the $15,000 we'll earn with sports bets. Nothing could be easier. Then you'll understand ...

To play double chance at roulette (red/black, 1-18/19-36, odd/even) you have to follow this strategy. You look at the last 35/40 numbers released to see if there are pairs of colors or triplets or quatrains, but also other double chances (odd and even, 1-18 and 19-36) if you have the patience to write the graph. In any case, for example, if we see a sequence like RR-BB - RR-NR-BB-RR-BB-RRRBR-BB-RR (R is red, B is black), as you notice there are many RR and BB pairs. The same could happen for the sequence of three or four consecutive colors. And so in the first case, we'll start playing two blacks and two reds without interruption (black black red red black black red red, etc.) applying the 30days progression with starting units based on the capital possessed. If there are more triplets we'll play three reds and three blacks. Starting the game sequence with blacks or reds is irrelevant but to do this I look if there are many consecutive in the last releases and then I play the opposite color released for last, or if there are more alternations then I play the same of the last one boules.

We'll play based on what has already come out because according to my theories the roulette is cyclical so if many couples or triplets are released it will be difficult for them to come out again and even if they happen again we only have one chance out of 4 of losing in the case of couples and one out of six in the case of triplets. I give you a practical demonstration (the asterisk indicates where you lost):

Played	Sequence 1	Sequence 2	Sequence 3	Sequence 4 (Loser)
Black	B	B	R*	R*
Black	B	R*	B	R*
Red	R	R	B*	B*
Red	R	B*	R	B*
Black	B	B	R*	R*
Black	B	R*	B	R*
Red	R	R	B*	B*
Red	R	B*	R	B*

With triplets and quatrains, it is more 'or less the same. In my opinion, however, the preferred sequence is always 2 reds and 2 blacks. The choice between pairs, triplets and quadruplets must also be made while we are playing based on the outputs. And of course, if you write the statistics of other double chances on a sheet, 1-18/19-36 and odd/even, you can do the same with these.

WE BEGIN

We'll play to the roulette with a start capital of $300 and will use the 30days progression with a starting chip of $2. A fundamental recommendation is to mark on a sheet of paper that you will prepare the last bet made in such a way as not to run into errors that could lead to disappointing defeats by mistake on a bet. To do this you will print sheets of paper with the various sequences, where you will go to mark the plays (see Attachments 1-2-3). So you will have a sheet with many sequences of RRBBRRBBRRBBRRBB etc, one with RRRBBBRRRBBBRRRBBB, etc, and one with RRRRBBBBRRRRBBBB, etc. Once you have made the stake, you will mark with a pen or pencil with the last color pointed in the sequence where you are so that you always know which color to point to the next round. On the bottom of the sheet, there are also written the individual numbers of the progression you are using, revalued based on the base unit, so you know how to increase and decrease the stake as you calculate based on the starting unit you are using 1, 2, 3, 4 or 5. If you are going up too much in the stake amount you can also increase less and decrease more in order not to burn the whole till and wait for a more favorable sequence.

If you have more economic possibilities and want to invest more can go directly to day 6 if they have $1000 available and on day 16 if you have $5,000.

LET'S PLAY

DAY 1

You enter to the roulette (when I say roulette it is understood that you'll play on European roulette single zero or without zero) with $300, to be increased by 24%, and you play with this economic progression based $2: 2,4,8 - 12,20,30,45,70,110. Come back to $2 if stake under $12 an two position in positive case if you stake more than $8, in this way you can resist 9 negative events. You'll do 3 sessions by +24$ active each (12 positive events x session) to reach $372. It will take in total less than an hour.

DAY 2

You enter to the roulette with $372 and play the same way as the day 1. You have to increase by $90 and you'll always do it in 3 sessions.

DAY 3

You enter the roulette with $462 but this time you play with base stake 3$ and 30days progression that is: 3,6,12 - 18,27,40,55,75,90,120 (you can round off some numbers for convenience), you can resist 10 negative events. You have to increase by $108 and you'll do it in 3 sessions of $36 each (12 positive events a sess.).

DAY 4

You enter to the roulette with $570 and play with a basic $4 chip that is: 4,8,16 - 24,36,50,70,100,140,200. You have to increase by $120 and you'll always do it in 3 sessions of $40 each (10 positive events x sess.).

DAY 5

You enter at the roulette with the $690 and you play with a base stake $4 like day 4. You have to increase by $120 and you'll do it in 3 sessions of $40 each (10 positive events x sess.).

DAY 6

You enter at the roulette with the $810 and you play with a base stake $4 like day 4. You have to increase by $120 and you'll do it in 3 sessions of $40 each (10 positive events x sess.).

DAYS FROM 7 TO 16.

You arrived around $930 capital, as already mentioned, in the next 10 days you have to reach $6100.

You enter to the Roulette with $450 and play with a $3 base. You have to win $120 a day and we'll do it in 3 sessions in which you have to have about 13/14 positive hits each.

The other money you'll win by betting staking the $480 remaining in this way: you'll divide it into 4 parts of $120 (who no longer wants to play roulette can divide all $930 into 7 parts from $130) and you'll stake them on a single or multiple a day with average odd variable from 1.90 to 2.10 which will give us the chosen Tipster or which you will find on my site www.30day30.webnode.it and you'll stake the whole sum back into play looking for a series of 3 consecutive victories that will make us increase the cash considerably (130->260->520->1040). You can also choose to do two bets with odd 3.00 as mentioned above but in this case, you have to win 4 times if you get both at least in one case (130 x1.5 x3 x1.5 x1.5 = $1,316).

You'll do this type of play because any good Tipster usually gets 4/5 consecutive doublings at least 3/4 times in a month and therefore the probability of getting 3 in a row is very high. To speed up the process you could play two times a day, one on matches that start in the early afternoon or morning and one on matches that start in the evening. Usually, the Tipster gives one of it in a day but you can find more multiples on my site. If you opt for one a day, just choose only one of the multiples published. When the capital will be increased you have to increase the base stake for the first doubling.

Said this you start with an initial stake of $130 on the first bet, single or multiple with odd about 2.00, if you win (130 x 2.00 = 260) you invest all the capital earned with this first bet in the second bet, if you win (260 x 2.00 = 520) you remove $80 and invest the rest of the winning in the third bet. At the third victory, you'll have (520-80 x 2.00 = 880). If you lose you try again with another $130 on the next bet chasing the 3 consecutive victories. If you decide to bet on odd about 1.50 (or 2 bets odd 3.00) you can find 4 consecutive wins. Meanwhile, we continue to earn $130 a day with roulette so that you always have the money to start betting on. It shouldn't be difficult, sometimes I've seen sequences of 7/8 consecutive wins, so it just takes a little patience. Once you get to $2000 you'll start staking $250 basic on the climb so you can increase the capital exponentially 250 x2.00x2.00(-150)x2.00 = $1700 or 250 x1.5 x3.0 x1.5(-250) x 1.5 = $2156). Arrived at $4000 you'll start the climb to stake base $500. You have 10/15 days to get to the $6100 we established but even if we had to put in a few more days we don't have to make a drama. Somebody will think that beginning $130 per day to try to climb is too many but in reality, the expense is much lower because you will lose the $130 only to the first try and not every day and therefore for example in 15 days, with bets by odd 2.00, you could have a situation like this the number is the day, the V indicates the wins and the X the defeat:

Cash $1100. 1st(-130)X. 2nd(-130)V. 3rdV. 4thV(1040). 5th(-130)V. 6thX. 7th(-130)V. 8thV. 9thV(1040). (1040+1040-130-130-130-130=+1560) Cash $2660. From this moment on we'll stake $250: 1st(-250)V. 2ndX. 3rd(-250)V. 4thV 5thV (2000). Cash $4160. From here we'll stake $500: 1st(-500)V. 2ndV(1000). Cash $4660.

In this case, therefore, was enough $520 which we had planned and 16 days to reach the goal and even exceed it.

Who doesn't love the roulette can skip the days from 1 to 5 and start with the $300 from the first day to look for the sequence of 3 consecutive wins to the bets starting from $50 so with 6 attempts available. Once the sum of $1100 is reached, you can start the program form the 6th and the following days. Certainly, in this way, you'll take longer than expected but you will get to the goal anyway.

Who is very practical and passionate about roulette can use this method of consecutive doubling even on roulette. That is if we divide the initial $300 into 30 parts by $10 we have 30 possible attempts to get 3 consecutive hits (as seen on page 16) for 9 times, which would mean going active. Beyond this method, which focuses on average winnings, we can also opt for an increase in the start sum in the event of a prolonged loss. When then the capital will be increased we can increase the initial stake, possibly stake 1/30th of the capital possessed.

DAYS FROM 17 TO 30

Once you reach the sum of $6100 you can withdraw $1100. Now you'll continue to play sport bets as in the past days, but this time looking for 4 consecutive victories starting from $500, if you remove $500 after the third doubling won you'll reach about $7000. If you win one of these series of 4 wins and two series of 3 wins you'll get the $15,000 that was missing. To do this you have available $5,000 so 10 attempts by $500. You could also stop at the third doubling for all climbs, in this case, you have to win 5 positive series and maybe it will take more than 30 days but you'll be even more sure of earning the $20,000.

In the following months, if you continue to stake $500/800 on doubling you can even stop at the second in a row because you have already multiplied the initial sum by 4. When you win 6 consecutive times you have won 3 sequences of 2 wins each so multiplied by 12 the start sum (500 x 12 = 6000). You can also play on the average monthly winnings that are generally higher than the losses, increasing a little if the losses last longer.

EARN FOR LIFE

At this point I believe that you have all become very capable of making money, so I don't have to tell you anything anymore, indeed some of your students as often happens, will be able to give me advice to win more than I can. However, I advise doing as I do, that is to look for 2/3 consecutive wins to the bets starting from $600 on doubling but increasing in case of prolonged losses to recover and to have an average monthly high enough winnings and therefore a profit of $15000/16000. Beyond this, I don't disdain to search series of 5/6 consecutive doubling starting from $100/150 and get even +$10,000 a couple of times a month. To do all this I sometimes stay for a few days around the country so that I can play in the betting offices of other cities and not always in those in my area that might otherwise cause me problems. Sometimes, to win at roulette, I visit real casinos that always give that extra thrill. So I just have to wish you .... **SO MUCH HAPPINESS!**

Attached 1

B B R R B B R R B B R R B B R R B B R R B B R R B B R R B B R R

B B R R B B R R B B R R B B R R B B R R B B R R B B R R B B R R

B B R R B B R R B B R R B B R R B B R R B B R R B B R R B B R R

B B R R B B R R B B R R B B R R B B R R B B R R B B R R B B R R

B B R R B B R R B B R R B B R R B B R R B B R R B B R R B B R R

B B R R B B R R B B R R B B R R B B R R B B R R B B R R B B R R

B B R R B B R R B B R R B B R R B B R R B B R R B B R R B B R R

B B R R B B R R B B R R B B R R B B R R B B R R B B R R B B R R

B B R R B B R R B B R R B B R R B B R R B B R R B B R R B B R R

B B R R B B R R B B R R B B R R B B R R B B R R B B R R B B R R

B B R R B B R R B B R R B B R R B B R R B B R R B B R R B B R R

B B R R B B R R B B R R B B R R B B R R B B R R B B R R B B R R

B B R R B B R R B B R R B B R R B B R R B B R R B B R R B B R R

B B R R B B R R B B R R B B R R B B R R B B R R B B R R B B R R

B B R R B B R R B B R R B B R R B B R R B B R R B B R R B B R R

B B R R B B R R B B R R B B R R B B R R B B R R B B R R B B R R

B B R R B B R R B B R R B B R R B B R R B B R R B B R R B B R R

B B R R B B R R B B R R B B R R B B R R B B R R B B R R B B R R

B B R R B B R R B B R R B B R R B B R R B B R R B B R R B B R R

1,2,4,8 - 13,20,30,45,67,100
2,4,8,16 - 25,40,60,90,130,200
3,6,12,24 - 40,60,90,130,200,300
4,8,16,32 - 50,80,120,180,260,400
5,10,20,40 - 60,100,150,225,335,500

Attached 2

BBB RRR BBB RRR BBB RRR BBB RRR BBB RRR BBB RRR BBB
RRR BBB RRR BBB RRR BBB RRR BBB RRR BBB RRR BBB RRR
BBB RRR BBB RRR BBB RRR BBB RRR BBB RRR BBB RRR BBB
RRR BBB RRR BBB RRR BBB RRR BBB RRR BBB RRR BBB RRR
BBB RRR BBB RRR BBB RRR BBB RRR BBB RRR BBB RRR BBB
RRR BBB RRR BBB RRR BBB RRR BBB RRR BBB RRR BBB RRR
BBB RRR BBB RRR BBB RRR BBB RRR BBB RRR BBB RRR BBB
RRR BBB RRR BBB RRR BBB RRR BBB RRR BBB RRR BBB RRR
BBB RRR BBB RRR BBB RRR BBB RRR BBB RRR BBB RRR BBB
RRR BBB RRR BBB RRR BBB RRR BBB RRR BBB RRR BBB RRR
BBB RRR BBB RRR BBB RRR BBB RRR BBB RRR BBB RRR BBB
RRR BBB RRR BBB RRR BBB RRR BBB RRR BBB RRR BBB RRR
BBB RRR BBB RRR BBB RRR BBB RRR BBB RRR BBB RRR BBB
RRR BBB RRR BBB RRR BBB RRR BBB RRR BBB RRR BBB RRR
BBB RRR BBB RRR BBB RRR BBB RRR BBB RRR BBB RRR BBB
RRR BBB RRR BBB RRR BBB RRR BBB RRR BBB RRR BBB RRR
BBB RRR BBB RRR BBB RRR BBB RRR BBB RRR BBB RRR BBB
RRR BBB RRR BBB RRR BBB RRR BBB RRR BBB RRR BBB RRR
BBB RRR BBB RRR BBB RRR BBB RRR BBB RRR BBB RRR BBB

1,2,4,8 - 13,20,30,45,67,100
2,4,8,16 - 25,40,60,90,130,200
3,6,12,24 - 40,60,90,130,200,300
4,8,16,32 - 50,80,120,180,260,400
5,10,20,40 - 60,100,150,225,335,500

Attached 3

BBBB RRRR BBBB RRRR BBBB RRRR BBBB RRRR BBBB RRRR

BBBB RRRR BBBB RRRR BBBB RRRR BBBB RRRR BBBB RRRR

BBBB RRRR BBBB RRRR BBBB RRRR BBBB RRRR BBBB RRRR

BBBB RRRR BBBB RRRR BBBB RRRR BBBB RRRR BBBB RRRR

BBBB RRRR BBBB RRRR BBBB RRRR BBBB RRRR BBBB RRRR

BBBB RRRR BBBB RRRR BBBB RRRR BBBB RRRR BBBB RRRR

BBBB RRRR BBBB RRRR BBBB RRRR BBBB RRRR BBBB RRRR

BBBB RRRR BBBB RRRR BBBB RRRR BBBB RRRR BBBB RRRR

BBBB RRRR BBBB RRRR BBBB RRRR BBBB RRRR BBBB RRRR

BBBB RRRR BBBB RRRR BBBB RRRR BBBB RRRR BBBB RRRR

BBBB RRRR BBBB RRRR BBBB RRRR BBBB RRRR BBBB RRRR

BBBB RRRR BBBB RRRR BBBB RRRR BBBB RRRR BBBB RRRR

BBBB RRRR BBBB RRRR BBBB RRRR BBBB RRRR BBBB RRRR

BBBB RRRR BBBB RRRR BBBB RRRR BBBB RRRR BBBB RRRR

BBBB RRRR BBBB RRRR BBBB RRRR BBBB RRRR BBBB RRRR

BBBB RRRR BBBB RRRR BBBB RRRR BBBB RRRR BBBB RRRR

BBBB RRRR BBBB RRRR BBBB RRRR BBBB RRRR BBBB RRRR

BBBB RRRR BBBB RRRR BBBB RRRR BBBB RRRR BBBB RRRR

BBBB RRRR BBBB RRRR BBBB RRRR BBBB RRRR BBBB RRRR

1,2,4,8 - 13,20,30,45,67,100
2,4,8,16 - 25,40,60,90,130,200
3,6,12,24 - 40,60,90,130,200,300
4,8,16,32 - 50,80,120,180,260,400
5,10,20,40 - 60,100,150,225,335,500